ANCIENT EGYPTIANS

AT A GLANCE

RUPERT MATTHEWS

MACDONALD YOUNG BOOKS

First published in Great Britain in 1998
by Macdonald Young Books
© Macdonald Young Books 1998

Macdonald Young Books, an imprint of
Wayland Publishers Limited
61 Western Road, Hove
East Sussex BN3 1JD

Find Macdonald Young Books on the Internet
at http://www.wayland.co.uk

Designed by: The Design Works, Reading
Edited by: Lisa Edwards
Illustrated by: Maltings Partnership

A CIP catalogue for this book is available from
the British Library.

Printed in Hong Kong by
Wing King Tong

ISBN: 0 7500 2400 3 HB

Other titles in the series:
Ancient Greeks
Ancient Romans
The Vikings

CONTENTS

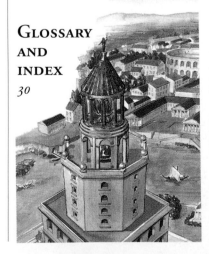

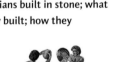

TIME TRACK

A DIVIDED HISTORY

In the third century BC, an Egyptian priest named Manetho wrote a history of Egypt. He divided Egyptian history into dynasties, or families of pharaohs. Modern historians grouped together dynasties that had features in common, such as government systems, into periods and kingdoms. Manetho did not know the exact dates of the earlier pharaohs, so he guessed. Archaeologists have discovered some early dates, but others are still unknown. ▼

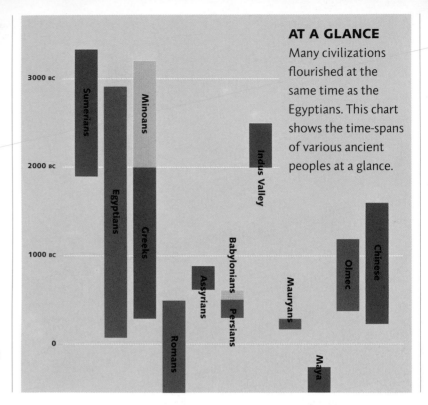

AT A GLANCE
Many civilizations flourished at the same time as the Egyptians. This chart shows the time-spans of various ancient peoples at a glance.

	EVENTS IN EGYPT	AROUND THE WORLD
	First farmers appear in Egypt 7000 BC **First towns settled** 4000 BC **Sails first used on boats on the Nile** c.4000 BC	**Earliest copperworking, Middle East** 7000 BC **Cereal farming begins in Europe** 6500 BC **Rice cultivation begins in Thailand** 6000 BC **Millet farming begins in China** 6000 BC
3500 BC	**Settlement and tombs at Hierakonpolis** c.3400 BC	**First city in China at Liang-ch'eng chen** 3500 BC **Foundation of city of Ur in Mesopotamia** 3500 BC
3000 BC	**Egypt unified under the first pharaoh, Menes** 3050 BC **Hieroglyphs develop from earlier picture writing** c.3000 BC **Papyrus first used for writing** c.2900 BC	**First vehicles with wheels appear in Mesopotamia** c.3000 BC **Stone structures built at Stonehenge, England** c.2800 BC **Indus Valley civilization begins in Pakistan** 2750 BC
2500 BC	**Step pyramid of Djoser built** c.2650 BC **Khufu builds Great Pyramid at Giza** 2530 BC	

Predynastic Period

Archaic Period
1st and 2nd Dynasties

Old Kingdom

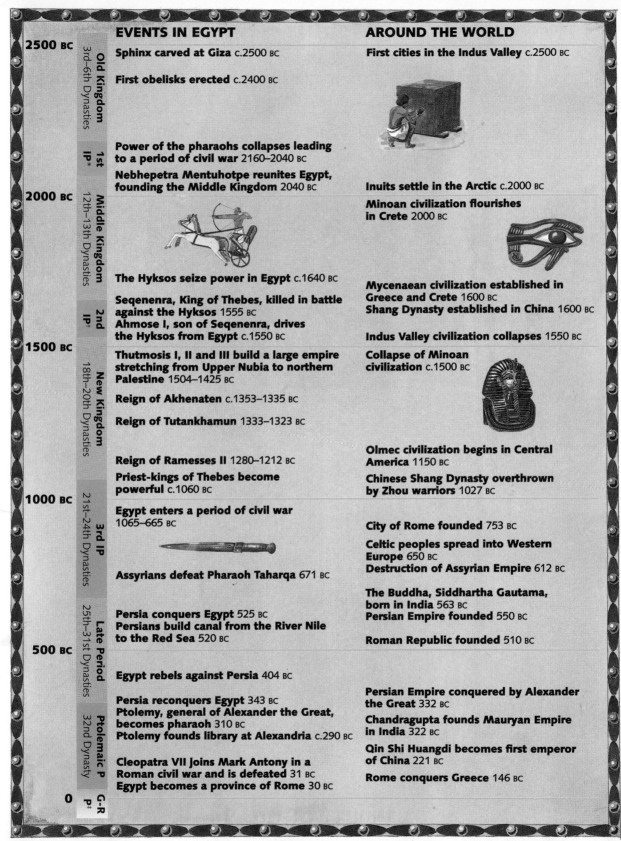

		EVENTS IN EGYPT	AROUND THE WORLD

2500 BC

Old Kingdom 3rd–6th Dynasties

Sphinx carved at Giza c.2500 BC

First cities in the Indus Valley c.2500 BC

First obelisks erected c.2400 BC

1st IP*

Power of the pharaohs collapses leading to a period of civil war 2160–2040 BC

Nebhepetra Mentuhotpe reunites Egypt, founding the Middle Kingdom 2040 BC

Inuits settle in the Arctic c.2000 BC

2000 BC

Middle Kingdom 12th–13th Dynasties

Minoan civilization flourishes in Crete 2000 BC

The Hyksos seize power in Egypt c.1640 BC

2nd IP†

Seqenenra, King of Thebes, killed in battle against the Hyksos 1555 BC

Ahmose I, son of Seqenenra, drives the Hyksos from Egypt c.1550 BC

Mycenaean civilization established in Greece and Crete 1600 BC

Shang Dynasty established in China 1600 BC

Indus Valley civilization collapses 1550 BC

1500 BC

New Kingdom 18th–20th Dynasties

Thutmosis I, II and III build a large empire stretching from Upper Nubia to northern Palestine 1504–1425 BC

Collapse of Minoan civilization c.1500 BC

Reign of Akhenaten c.1353–1335 BC

Reign of Tutankhamun 1333–1323 BC

Reign of Ramesses II 1280–1212 BC

Olmec civilization begins in Central America 1150 BC

Priest-kings of Thebes become powerful c.1060 BC

Chinese Shang Dynasty overthrown by Zhou warriors 1027 BC

1000 BC

3rd IP 21st–24th Dynasties

Egypt enters a period of civil war 1065–665 BC

City of Rome founded 753 BC

Celtic peoples spread into Western Europe 650 BC

Destruction of Assyrian Empire 612 BC

Assyrians defeat Pharaoh Taharqa 671 BC

The Buddha, Siddhartha Gautama, born in India 563 BC

Persian Empire founded 550 BC

Late Period 25th–31st Dynasties

Persia conquers Egypt 525 BC

Persians build canal from the River Nile to the Red Sea 520 BC

Roman Republic founded 510 BC

500 BC

Egypt rebels against Persia 404 BC

Persia reconquers Egypt 343 BC

Persian Empire conquered by Alexander the Great 332 BC

Ptolemaic P 32nd Dynasty

Ptolemy, general of Alexander the Great, becomes pharaoh 310 BC

Ptolemy founds library at Alexandria c.290 BC

Chandragupta founds Mauryan Empire in India 322 BC

Qin Shi Huangdi becomes first emperor of China 221 BC

Cleopatra VII joins Mark Antony in a Roman civil war and is defeated 31 BC

Egypt becomes a province of Rome 30 BC

Rome conquers Greece 146 BC

0

G-R P‡

---

* **1st Intermediate Period** 7th–11th Dynasties   † **2nd Intermediate Period** 14th–17th Dynasties   ‡ **Graeco-Roman Period**

Site-seeing – A Guide to Ancient Egypt

For nearly three thousand years Egypt was one of the richest and most powerful nations on earth. Under the rule of the pharaoh 'god-kings', the Egyptians built gigantic pyramids, enormous temples and colossal statues, and gathered vast treasures of gold and jewels. All this wealth and power relied on the River Nile. Each year the Nile flooded the narrow valley and wide delta, leaving a thick layer of fertile mud in which crops grew easily. Beyond the reach of the floods stretched the desert where nothing would grow. Ancient Egypt depended on the Nile and most of the sites in the kingdom are crowded along its length.

Avaris was the capital of the 15th Dynasty Hyksos kings. The Hyksos wanted a city that was near to their homeland, to the northeast of the Sinai desert.

 Bubastis was the home town of the 22nd Dynasty. These pharaohs built a huge temple to their favourite goddess, the cat Bastet. Bastet was famous for her annual festival, which involved long, riotous parties.

Tanis was a small city that became the capital of Ancient Egypt during the 21st and 22nd Dynasties. This occurred during a period of civil war.

Lower Egypt contained the Nile Delta and was one of the two large kingdoms united by the 1st Dynasty. It was symbolized by the red crown, the *deshret*.

Map

N

MEDITERRANEAN SEA

• Avaris

• Tanis

Bubastis

Cairo

Memphis

Giza Sakkara

Leontopolis

LOWER EGYPT

RIVER NILE

Akhetaten

FAYUM Hermopolis

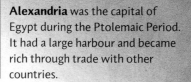

Alexandria

 Giza is a plateau on the edge of the desert near Memphis. The giant pyramids of the 4th Dynasty were built here, as was the Sphinx.

Alexandria was the capital of Egypt during the Ptolemaic Period. It had a large harbour and became rich through trade with other countries.

Memphis stood near the junction of Upper and Lower Egypt. Most pharaohs lived in Memphis and ran the country from here.

Sakkara was the site of royal monuments during the Archaic Period. The first pyramid was built here for Pharaoh Djoser.

8

Leontopolis was a massive fortress surrounded by huge walls. It was built by the Hyksos, but continued to be used by the New Kingdom pharaohs.

 The city of **Akhetaten** was built by the 18th Dynasty pharaoh Akhenaten. He worshipped a new god, Aten, and built this entirely new city to replace Thebes, which was dedicated to the god Amun.

Aswan was the most southern city of Ancient Egypt. Its quarries supplied granite for many Egyptian monuments. In 1970, a huge dam was constructed across the Nile at Aswan.

 Thebes (modern-day Luxor) was the ceremonial and religious centre of Egypt in the New Kingdom. The pharaoh came to Thebes to worship the great god Amun and to carry out important sacred ceremonies.

Abydos was the centre for the worship of the god Osiris, whose tomb is said to be here. Some early pharaohs were buried here to be close to him.

 Kom Ombo was the site of a temple to Sobek, the crocodile god. The temple was entirely rebuilt in the Ptolemaic Period.

The **First Cataract** is a set of rapids at Elephantine. Egyptian boats could not sail up the rapids and so these marked the southern limit of Egypt.

Thebes   Kom Ombo   Aswan

Edfu   Elephantine

VALLEY OF THE KINGS   **FIRST CATARACT**   RIVER NILE   **NUBIA**

•Abydos

UPPER EGYPT

Abu Simbel •

Fayum is a low-lying, marshy area. In ancient times it was the site of a lake and farm land.

Hermopolis was a very important city from the Middle Kingdom onwards. Thousands of baboons were mummified and buried here, near to the temple of Thoth.

 Upper Egypt contained the Nile valley from Elephantine to Sakkara. It was the more powerful of the two predynastic kingdoms and was symbolized by the white crown, the *hedjet*.

Edfu was a fortified city from the Old Kingdom onwards, and was a major defence against invading Nubians. The temple of Horus at Edfu is one of the best preserved of all the Ancient Egyptian temples.

 The **Valley of the Kings** lies west of Thebes. The pharaohs of the New Kingdom, including Tutankhamun, were buried here in magnificent underground tombs.

Elephantine was a sacred island in the Nile. A predynastic temple there was enlarged in the Old Kingdom and then rebuilt during the 18th Dynasty. This shrine remained in use for nearly 3,000 years.

 **Abu Simbel** was the site of two massive rock temples carved by Ramesses II to show he had conquered Nubia. The temples were moved to high ground in 1965 to avoid being flooded by the new Lake Nasser.

THE WEALTH OF THE NILE

Without the River Nile, life in Egypt would not be possible. Ancient Egyptians depended on the rich harvests that the yearly flood in the valley would bring. Some of the pharaoh's most important duties were conducting religious ceremonies to ensure a good harvest. Most people lived and worked on the fertile farm land around the Nile, and traded their produce along its banks.

THE FARMING YEAR

The farming year in Egypt began in October as the Nile flood ended. Wheat and barley were sown at once, while the ground was still soft. The harvest began in the following March. Farmers not only worked the land, they also had to work for the pharaoh. They mended canals and ditches, worked on building projects and fought in the army. ▼

THE NILE ROAD

Once Upper and Lower Egypt were united, merchants used the Nile for trading. Most trade was between places in Egypt. Food was shipped from farm land to the cities. Stone from Aswan was moved by boat for use in temples and tombs. A few merchants traded outside Egypt. In Nubia, Egyptian merchants exchanged food and other products for ivory, ostrich feathers and fur skins. In the Nile Delta, they traded with Syrians for silver and timber and with Greeks for pottery.

CONTROLLING THE NILE

The Ancient Egyptians built a network of canals and ditches to carry the river water to the fields. This network was used to store the water when the floods had gone. In most years the Egyptians grew more food than they could eat. Spare food was sold to other countries and Egypt grew wealthy.

1 In the time of inundation (July to October) people moved to higher ground to avoid the floods. They fished from papyrus-reed boats. Farmers had to go to work for the pharaoh, building temples and pyramids.

2 In the time of emergence (November to February) the floods receded. Oxen pulled wooden ploughs through the rich, black Nile mud. Men scattered the seed. Animals were herded along behind to tread it into the soil.

3 During the growing season farmers were busy. Crops had to be weeded. Water had to be carried to the fields from canals, ditches, tanks, or from the Nile. Farmers watched over their crops and threw stones to scare the birds.

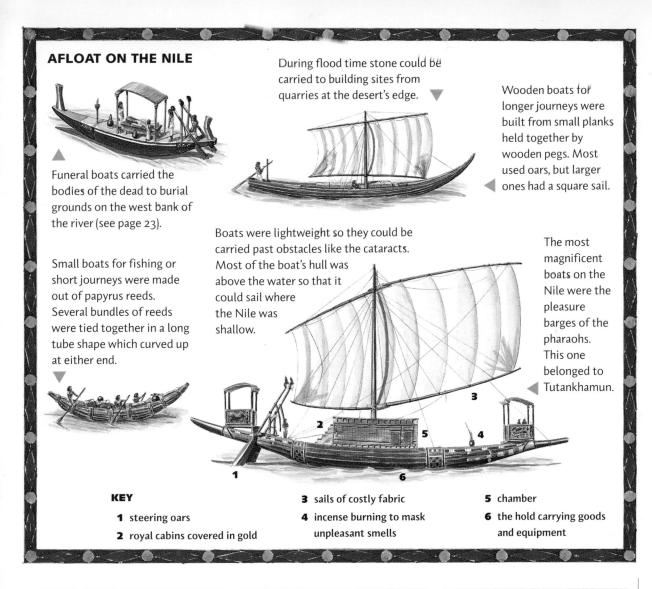

AFLOAT ON THE NILE

Funeral boats carried the bodies of the dead to burial grounds on the west bank of the river (see page 23).

During flood time stone could be carried to building sites from quarries at the desert's edge.

Wooden boats for longer journeys were built from small planks held together by wooden pegs. Most used oars, but larger ones had a square sail.

Small boats for fishing or short journeys were made out of papyrus reeds. Several bundles of reeds were tied together in a long tube shape which curved up at either end.

Boats were lightweight so they could be carried past obstacles like the cataracts. Most of the boat's hull was above the water so that it could sail where the Nile was shallow.

The most magnificent boats on the Nile were the pleasure barges of the pharaohs. This one belonged to Tutankhamun.

KEY

1 steering oars
2 royal cabins covered in gold

3 sails of costly fabric
4 incense burning to mask unpleasant smells

5 chamber
6 the hold carrying goods and equipment

4 In the time of harvest (March to June) reapers cut the corn using wooden sickles with sharp flint edges. Gleaners followed behind making sure that every ear of corn was picked up. This job was left to women and children.

5 The ears of corn were trampled by animals or hit with flails on a stone threshing floor to separate the grain from the chaff (husks). Then the grain was tossed in the air so the chaff would blow away. This was called winnowing.

6 Grain was stored in granaries. It was poured in through a hole in the roof. When it was needed it was taken out through doors at the bottom. Scribes watched carefully to check that the pharaoh got his share of every crop.

FAMOUS PHARAOHS

THE LIVING GOD

Egyptians believed the first pharaohs to be the children, or the representatives, of gods. It was thought that only the pharaoh could cause the Nile to flood and the farm animals to produce offspring and milk. The pharaoh had to carry out special ceremonies to ensure the health and happiness of his people. The pharaoh was worshipped and obeyed by his people because they believed that their own health depended on him.

Sceptres were carried by pharaohs and gods as symbols of their authority.

Sekhem

Flail

Crook

CROWNING GLORY

The earliest pharaohs of Upper Egypt wore a white crown and kings of Lower Egypt wore a red crown. Later pharaohs wore the double crown of a united Egypt. Sometimes pharaohs wore the *Atef* crown of Osiris or a smaller blue crown decorated with a vulture and a snake. These creatures symbolized the Delta and the upper Nile valley. ▶

THE PHARAOH: KING AND GOD

Pharaohs ordered palaces, temples and pyramids to be built, to honour themselves and other gods. They travelled around their kingdom, checking what was being done in their name.

KEY

1 double crown	**3** flail	**6** fan bearer
2 crook	**4** litter	**7** ostrich-feather fan
	5 porter	**8** pyramid being built

ALL THE KINGS' NAMES

Every pharaoh had several names apart from his personal name. Pharaohs often added phrases mentioning the names of the gods they were related to and took a special name when they became rulers. These names would be carved on their tombs and funeral temples. It is not surprising that archaeologists often have difficulty deciding which name refers to which pharaoh!

These two *cartouches* give the name of Horemheb in hieroglyphs (see page 24).

White crown **Red crown** **Double crown** **Atef crown** **Blue crown**

12

Nebhepetra Mentuhotpe reunited Egypt in 2065 BC, founding both the 11th Dynasty and the Middle Kingdom. He had fought a vicious civil war with other Egyptian rulers to unite the country, then had led an army to reconquer Nubia. He built a large tomb-temple to the west of Thebes. ▶

Tutankhamun came to the throne in 1333 BC at the age of eight. He worshipped the god Amun and returned the treasures taken from Amun's temples by his father, Akhenaten. He died aged 17 and is famous for his magnificent tomb, discovered in 1922.

◀ **Hatshepsut**, wife of Thutmosis II, became the strongest ruler of the New Kingdom. When her husband died in 1479 BC, her ten-year-old son was left to rule Egypt. However, real power lay with Hatshepsut. She declared herself pharaoh and is often shown in male clothing, wearing a beard.

Akhenaten tried to change the entire religion of Egypt. When he came to power in 1353 BC, the priests of Amun in Thebes controlled much of Egypt's wealth. Akhenaten stripped the priests of their wealth and power, and built a new sacred city dedicated to the god Aten. ▶

◀ **Ramesses II** ruled a great empire from Syria to southern Nubia from about 1280 BC to 1212 BC. The taxes from the empire gave Egypt immense wealth. Ramesses built some of the most famous buildings in Ancient Egypt, including the temples of Abu Simbel and the Ramesseum.

WHO RULED EGYPT?

Archaic Period	1st and 2nd Dynasties	**Menes** c.3050 BC
		Khasekhemui c.2700 BC
Old Kingdom	3rd–6th Dynasties	**Djoser** 2652–2635 BC
		Sneferu 2598–2545 BC
		Khufu 2515–2492 BC
		Pepy II 2290–2195 BC
1st Middle Kingdom	IP* 12th–13th Dyn.	**Inyotef I** 2160–2122 BC
		Khety 2100 BC
		Nebhepetra Mentuhotpe 2065–2013 BC
		Senwosret III 1878–1841 BC
2nd		**Hor** 1740 BC
IP†		**Apophis** c.1585–1545 BC
New Kingdom	18th–20th Dynasties	**Ahmose** 1550–1525 BC
		Hatshepsut 1473–1458 BC
		Akhenaten 1353–1335 BC
		Tutankhamun 1333–1323 BC
		Horemheb 1329–1300 BC
		Ramesses II 1280–1212 BC
3rd IP	21st–24th Dyn.	**Smendes** 1063–1039 BC
		Shoshenq I 945–924 BC
		Osorkon IV 732–715 BC
Late Period	25th–31st Dyn.	**Taharqa** 690–664 BC
		Necho II 610–595 BC
		Darius I 521–486 BC
Ptolemaic P	32nd Dynasty	**Ptolemy I** 310–281 BC
		Ptolemy IV 221–204 BC
		Cleopatra VII 51–30 BC

Timeline markers: 3000 BC, 2500 BC, 2000 BC, 1500 BC, 1000 BC, 500 BC, 0

* **1st Intermediate Period** 7th–11th Dynasties
† **2nd Intermediate Period** 14th–17th Dynasties

13

EGYPTIAN SOCIETY

Ancient Egyptian society was divided into very distinct ranks of people. It was thought that the gods gave people their position. Temple priests were very highly respected citizens, and scribes and officials were honoured because they could read and write.

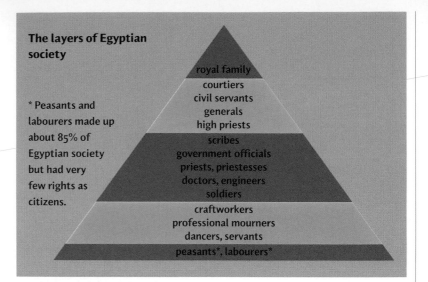

The layers of Egyptian society

* Peasants and labourers made up about 85% of Egyptian society but had very few rights as citizens.

royal family
courtiers
civil servants
generals
high priests

scribes
government officials
priests, priestesses
doctors, engineers
soldiers

craftworkers
professional mourners
dancers, servants

peasants*, labourers*

Chasing a thief

Traders using the deben system

TOWNS AND VILLAGES

Most people lived in towns and villages, in houses built of mud brick. Houses were often several storeys high and packed close together, with narrow streets and alleys running in-between. Wealthy nobles had houses with large central courtyards and many rooms. Their gardens had pools filled with fish and exotic plants. Poorer people lived in just a few rooms shared with other families. Towns and villages often grew up around the sites of new temples.

THE LAW

Egypt had strict laws based on the teachings of the gods and priests. Local men were expected to help chase and catch criminals, although soldiers were used to fight gangs. Cases were tried by judges who were usually local landowners or priests. They prayed to the gods for help in reaching the right decision. Criminals were beaten, whipped, sent to work at the temple or executed.

MONEY

The early Egyptians did not use money. Instead they simply swapped things. By the time of the New Kingdom, a system of payment called *deben* had been invented. A deben was a weight of copper. Every object for sale was given a value in deben by a scribe. A person wishing to buy a coffin worth 25 deben might offer three pigs, worth 5 deben each, and five goats, worth 2 deben each. Coins were first used in about 300 BC.

EDUCATION

Most Egyptian children did not go to school. Boys learned how to farm or work at a trade from their fathers. Girls learned how to cook and run a household from their mothers. Children from rich families went to school to learn to read. Often these schools were run by a temple. Rich boys were taught mathematics, medicine and other skills as well as writing. Later they often went on to become government officials or priests. ▶

WOMEN IN EGYPT

Some women had important rights and duties. Some became priestesses and a few royal princesses became pharaohs. Women often worked as musicians or dancers but most of them were expected to run the family household. When a man went to join the army or work on a building project, his wife was left in charge of their land and goods. Women kept control of their own property and neither their fathers nor their husbands could question their authority.

WORKING FOR THE PHARAOH

The craftspeople of Ancient Egypt were highly skilled and could produce delicate pieces of work. As time passed, they developed new skills and techniques. Most craftspeople worked in small workshops run by a temple or a wealthy landowner. Only a few foreign workers owned their own workshops. The pharaoh might order hundreds of craftspeople to move to a new town to work on an important project.

Metalworkers were highly respected. At first they worked only in gold and copper, but by the New Kingdom, they had discovered how to make bronze. Ironworking was developed later by copying skills from the Hittites.

Carpenters used tools of copper and stone. Wood was scarce in Egypt, so the carpenters became skilled at joining small pieces together to make large objects.

EVERYDAY LIFE

Egyptians worked hard, but they loved to play games and sports whenever they had some spare time. Some religious festivals involved playing games and performing sacred dances.

FESTIVALS AND FEASTING

Rich Egyptians loved to entertain their friends with food, music and dancing. Everyone celebrated occasions such as religious festivals, or the crowning of a pharaoh.

Professional musicians were hired to play at parties or to keep workers amused. They played many different instruments.

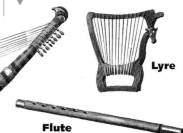

Harp

Lyre

Flute

Dance played an important part in religious festivals and at banquets. Most dancers were women. Some performed acrobatics as part of their act.

FOOD AND DRINK

Most Egyptians made their own food from crops and animals raised on their farms. Some food was produced by specialist craftspeople. Bakers made bread using wheat or barley flour. Beer was made from barley in breweries. It needed to be stored in cool cellars. After the New Kingdom, vineyards produced wine.

Beer Beans Ox

Melons Lentils

Milk

Fish Leeks

Honey

Onions

Lettuce

Garlic

Wine

Figs Grapes Dates

Pomegranates

Cucumber

Duck Goose

Egyptian potters made bowls and dishes with simple round shapes. Wine was kept in jars sealed with lumps of clay.

CLOTHES AND JEWELLERY

Egypt is a very hot, dry country. Most clothes were made of cool linen. Children often wore no clothes at all because of the heat. In winter, woollen cloaks kept people warm. Egyptians cared a great deal about their appearance. Men and women of all social classes wore make-up.

1 People often shaved their heads and bodies. Wigs were made of wool or human hair, fixed together with beeswax.

2 Perfume cones on wigs melted when warm, allowing sweet, oily perfume to run down over women's shoulders.

3 Men wore short kilts.

4 Women wore long dresses.

5 The Egyptians discovered how to make pleats in fabric, using starch to hold them in place.

Polished copper mirror and comb

Royal bracelet

Sandals were often made of leather or straw. Priests were only allowed to wear sandals made of reeds.

Gold ring with scarab-shaped swivelling top carved from steatite (soapstone)

This ornate pectoral was worn on the chest.

The jewellers of Ancient Egypt were among the finest of their time. They used gold from mines in the desert and in Nubia, and coloured stones such as garnets and lapis lazuli. Poorer people had jewellery made of shells, pottery and copper. People were buried with their jewellery so that they could use it in the afterlife (see page 22).

CHILDREN AT PLAY

At cool times of the day children came out to play. Their model animals and dolls were made of wood and ivory. Ball games were also popular.

Toy wooden horse with wheels

Girls playing 'catch' on each other's backs

BOARD GAMES

Board games have been found in the earliest tombs. All Egyptians played games, especially *hounds and jackals* and *senet*.

Hounds and jackals was played with small pegs carved with the heads of hounds and jackals. The pegs fitted into a board studded with holes.

HUNTING

Wealthy Egyptians loved to go hunting. They used chariots in the desert to hunt wild animals. On the Nile, they caught birds, fish and animals from boats.

Hunting for crocodiles and hippopotami

GODS AND GODDESSES

The Egyptians believed in many gods and goddesses. Some were gods of a particular thing or activity, others were patron gods of towns and places. Over time, some gods changed their nature, some were forgotten and others became more important. Egyptian religion was constantly changing as people adapted it to help them understand the changing world around them.

The bodies of sacred animals were mummified, just like those of people.

TEMPLES: HOUSES OF THE GODS

The Egyptians built temples as houses for their gods. At the centre of each temple was a small dark room called a sanctuary. Inside was the temple statue. People thought that the spirit of a god lived in its statue. Only the chief priest and pharaoh were allowed to enter the sanctuary. Three times a day one of them washed the statue, dressed it and gave it a meal. People left food at the temple for the god to eat.

Each god or goddess had a festival day. On festival days the statue was brought out of the temple and carried past the crowds in a procession.

KEY

1 priests carrying fans

2 musicians and singers

3 priests carrying the shrine

4 sacred *barque* (model boat) on which the shrine was often carried

5 golden shrine with statue inside, covered to hide it from the eyes of ordinary people

Ra,
sun god who created the world

Amun-Ra,
king of the gods. God of creation

Set,
god of war, deserts and storms

Anubis,
jackal-headed god of embalming

Sekhmet,
goddess of war and disease

Hathor,
goddess of music, dancing and happiness

THE OSIRIS MYTH

Osiris was one of the most popular gods of Egypt. He was god of farming, death and rebirth. Egyptians believed that Osiris had once ruled Egypt as a pharaoh, but was murdered by his jealous brother Set, god of deserts, storms and war. Set cut up the body of Osiris and hid the pieces. Osiris' wife, Isis, found the pieces, put them back together and conceived a son, Horus. Horus, the hawk god of the day and the air, defeated Set and became the new pharaoh. After this, Osiris became king of the dead. Isis was the goddess of magic and life.

Horus

Osiris   **Isis**

SACRED ANIMALS

Egyptian gods are often shown as humans with animal heads. Real animals were kept in some temples. People thought they were the living forms of gods. When the animals died they were mummified and buried in tombs like the pharaohs (see pages 22 and 23).

CHANGING GODS

Until the 18th Dynasty pharaohs were believed to be the children of the chief god, the sun god Ra. Then priests and pharaohs began to worship the sky god Amun as chief god. Later, they decided that Amun and Ra were two forms of the same god of the sky, and created a new god called Amun-Ra. The pharaohs could then continue to be called children of the chief god of Egypt.

Statues like this one, of the ram of Amun protecting the pharaoh, line the approach to the temple at Karnak.

THE PRIESTS

Every temple had priests. Their job was to carry out religious ceremonies, look after the temple and help ordinary people with sacred works. The High Priest and a few of his helpers were full-time priests. However, most priests worked for only a few months of the year. The rest of the time they were merchants or workmen. Priests shaved their heads and bodies every day and inhaled incense to wash away the ordinary world.

Sobek, god of the waters. Usually shown as a crocodile

Bastet, goddess of joy and motherhood. Shown as a cat

Khnum, ram-headed god who created babies out of clay. God of potters

Thoth, moon god who taught humans how to write and count. Shown as a man with the head of an ibis bird

TEMPLES, TOMBS AND PYRAMIDS

The Ancient Egyptians were among the first people to build in stone. They erected huge temples, tombs and pyramids, which were among the biggest buildings in the ancient world. These were constructed so well that many have lasted for thousands of years.

FROM SAND TO STONE

1 The earliest burial places were holes in the sand. Later they had mounds on top.

2 Then, rectangular mud-brick tombs called *mastabas* developed.

3 The first pyramid was built for Pharaoh Djoser at Sakkara in about 2650 BC. It started out as a square mastaba. Later it was adapted to form a pyramid shape with a stepped surface.

BUILDING IN STONE

Blocks were chiselled with marks to identify them.

1 Craftsmen and labourers split and shaped huge blocks of stone in Egyptian quarries. Soft limestone and sandstone were split using wooden wedges and water. Harder stone, such as granite, was pounded into shape with balls of volcanic rock.

2 Finished blocks were loaded onto sledges. Oxen dragged them to the Nile for transportation by barge to the building site. Mud helped the sledges to slide along.

The block of stone at the tip of the pyramid is called the capstone.

Labourers polished the surface with rough stones until it shone.

3 The Egyptians built ramps of rubble to act as scaffolding. They pulled blocks of stone up them. As they built higher, they extended the ramps. As the pyramid was completed, they took the ramps down again. The work was very dangerous. ▶

Triangular casing blocks fitted on the steps of the pyramid to make the surface smooth.

Later pyramids, such as the Great Pyramid of Pharaoh Khufu at Giza, had smooth sides. This is the largest pyramid of all and it contains many burial chambers and passages – people think it would have taken 100,000 men about twenty-five years to build.

THE TEMPLES

At the centre of all Egyptian temples was the sanctuary, a small dark room in which a god was believed to live (see page 18). Halls and courtyards were built to allow religious processions out in a straight line from the sanctuary. Granaries, schools and storerooms surrounded the main building. The entrance to the temple had stone pylons (towers) and obelisks. Obelisks were pillars carved from single blocks of stone. They had pyramid-shaped tips. One obelisk stood over 36 metres tall and weighed 460 tonnes. Some temples were huge. The Temple of Amun at Thebes was over 300 metres square.

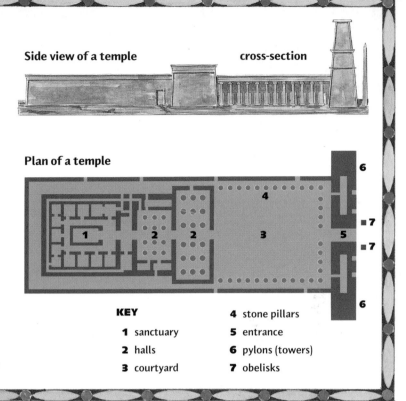

Side view of a temple   cross-section

Plan of a temple

KEY

1 sanctuary	**4** stone pillars
2 halls	**5** entrance
3 courtyard	**6** pylons (towers)
	7 obelisks

STATUES

Pharaohs often erected giant statues of themselves at temples and palaces. The temple of Abu Simbel was carved by Ramesses II out of a cliff on the banks of the River Nile in Nubia. The front of the temple is made up of four enormous statues of the pharaoh. ▼

PRECISION WORKING

Egyptian builders worked very accurately. They used dishes of water to make sure stones were level. If a stone was uneven, the water would slop out. String and wooden measures were used to check angles and heights. For large projects, builders used the positions of stars to help them.

Plumb line to check verticals

Chisel and mallet for chipping and splitting rocks

Wooden set square to check right angles

The string on a **bow drill** turned the drill when the wooden frame was pushed to and fro.

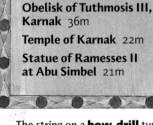

Adze for planing and smoothing wooden surfaces

HOW HIGH?

Great Pyramid, Giza 146m

Step pyramid of Djoser, Sakkara 62m

Obelisk of Tuthmosis III, Karnak 36m

Temple of Karnak 22m

Statue of Ramesses II at Abu Simbel 21m

THE LAND OF THE DEAD

One of the most important religious beliefs in Ancient Egypt was that people survived death. The earliest Egyptians were buried in the desert sands. The dry, hot sand preserved the bodies. Perhaps this is why the Egyptians came to believe their bodies had to be preserved (embalmed and mummified) if their spirits were to enjoy life in the land of the dead.

THE AFTERLIFE

From the time of the Old Kingdom it was believed that everyone would live on after they died. The afterlife was thought to take place in the

Amulet of the eye of Horus, who guided people through the afterlife.

Field of Reeds, which was just like Earth but much better. Farmers did not need to work the land, they could watch their crops grow while they played games. To enjoy the afterlife, two parts of a person's spirit had to be re-united with their body after death. These were called the 'ka' and 'ba'. This was why the preserving of dead bodies was thought so important.

Canopic jars held the dead person's internal organs. Each jar was different. The baboon-headed jar held the lungs, the falcon the intestines, the jackal the stomach, and the human-headed jar held the liver. The jars fitted into a cask.

Amulets were put between the layers of bandage around the mummy's body.

PREPARING FOR THE AFTERLIFE: MUMMIFICATION

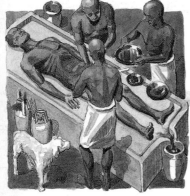

1 Embalming was skilled work. The dead body was laid on a stone slab. The internal organs were removed, except for the heart. The brains were thrown away. The other organs were dried out and put in Canopic jars in the tomb. The space left inside the body was packed with rags, sawdust or leaves scented with spices and herbs. Then it was stitched up again.

2 Next the body was covered with salt crystals called natron. It took up to 100 days for the natron to dry the body out. Once it was dried, it did not decay. Archaeologists know this because they have found mummified bodies in tombs, preserved almost perfectly to the present day.

3 The dried-out body was rubbed with fragrant oils and dressed in jewellery. Then it was wrapped tightly in hundreds of metres of linen bandages. Up to twenty layers were put on, each sealed with resin. The embalmers tucked magic amulets into the layers of bandage, to protect the body from evil. Last of all they bound a linen cloth, or shroud, in place. This slow process could take fifteen days.

READY FOR A NEW LIFE

People were buried with everything they might need in the afterlife. Food, wine, clothes, jewellery – all were sealed into the tomb. Sometimes a real boat was taken to pieces and rebuilt inside the tomb for a pharaoh to travel on. Often, models or pictures of objects were put in place of the real things. These were considered just as good, for symbolic purposes.

Model figures of servants, called *shabtis*, were included in tombs to do the pharaoh's work in the afterlife.

JOURNEY OF THE DEAD

The journey from Earth to the afterlife was long and difficult. First the spirit had to cross a wide river, then pass through gates guarded by monsters. Then it had to stand trial for any crimes it had committed on Earth. Next the spirit appeared before Osiris, king of the dead, in the Hall of the Two Truths. Anubis weighed the spirit's heart against the feather of the truth goddess Maat. If they weighed the same the spirit was allowed into the Field of Reeds. If not, the spirit was eaten by a crocodile and it was condemned to another death.

Anubis weighing the heart of a spirit against a feather. If the dead person had lived a life full of badness their heart would be heavier than the feather. This meant their spirit would not be able to go and live with the gods.

4 A mask painted with a likeness of the person was fixed to the shroud.

5 A mummy case (coffin) was made from wood or *cartonnage* (a sort of papier mâché). It was painted with hieroglyphs and brightly coloured pictures of the person's life, and spells to protect them in the afterlife. This inner case fitted inside one or more other decorated mummy cases.

6 Now the mummy was ready for the funeral ceremony. People generally lived on the east bank of the Nile, and the cemeteries were on the west bank. Mummies were dragged to the water's edge on a bier (sledge) pulled by oxen. They crossed the river on funeral boats (see page 11). The mummy was laid under a canopy on the boat. Two women mourners with shaved heads stood on either side, and an oarsman steered the boat.

7 At the tomb the ceremony of the 'opening of the mouth' was performed. A priest held up the mummy and the family touched it with special objects to allow it to see, hear and eat in the afterlife. Then it was taken into the tomb, along with everything it needed for the afterlife. Egyptians took great care in sealing up their tombs. But robbers often found ways in and stole the precious possessions that they found there.

WORDS AND PICTURES

The Egyptians invented a unique form of writing known as *hieroglyphics*. 'Hieroglyph' is a Greek word that means 'sacred writing in stone'. This sophisticated form of picture writing was painted and carved onto Egyptian temples, tombs and statues. Hieroglyphic writing died out during the third and fourth centuries AD, but the pictures that survive tell us much about aspects of life in Ancient Egypt.

PICTURE IDEAS

Hieroglyphs are pictures of objects. They can be read from left to right, or right to left, depending on the way the pictures face. Some hieroglyphs represent objects or ideas with pictures, but most represent the sounds of the Egyptian language. Pictures were put together to make sentences. To avoid confusion the Egyptians often used special symbols. For example, a person's name was always put into a box. Royal names were put in a *cartouche*, or oval box (see page 12).

'Ancient Egyptians' and 'At a glance' written in hieroglyphs ▼

UNDERSTANDING HIEROGLYPHS

The skill of reading hieroglyphs was lost by AD 500, and modern scholars could not understand them. Then a stone was found at Rosetta in Egypt which had the same inscription in Greek and hieroglyphic. The French scholar Jean Champollion spent years trying to crack the code of the strange Egyptian script. In 1824 he published a book that explained how hieroglyphs worked. It was several years before the meaning of all 750 pictures was solved.

Jean Champollion

The Rosetta Stone

THE SCRIPTS

Hieroglyphs were used for royal and sacred writings. They were carved and painted onto state monuments, temples, tombs and religious documents. A different script called *hieratic* was used by scribes for business contracts and letters. It was based on hieroglyphics, but each picture was simplified into a symbol so it could be written more quickly. Scribes wrote on a kind of paper made out of papyrus reeds.

▲
This text says 'Ancient Egyptians' in hieratic script

THE BOOK OF THE DEAD

Much of what we know about religion in Egypt comes from rolls of papyrus found in tombs. On the papyrus are sacred writings and spells copied by scribes from the *Book of the Dead*. This important religious book has 189 spells, though not everyone's version had all of the possible spells. Egyptians believed that these spells would help people in the afterlife. ▼

Ancient Egyptians

At a glance

EGYPTIAN ART

Egyptian art was used to put across messages. People and gods were shown holding symbolic objects and standing in a particular way so the messages would be understood. For example, if a pharaoh was shown dragging a prisoner by the hair and holding a club, this meant the pharaoh had won a battle.

Egyptian paintings show an object in the way it is clearest. The body is shown facing the front, but the legs are seen from the side. Artists drew grid patterns to help them give bodies the right proportions.

THE SCRIBES

Men who could read and write were called scribes. All priests and government officials were scribes. They needed to know how to read and write to keep records and send letters. Their writings help us to understand what life was like in Egypt.

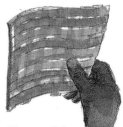

Basket of papyrus scrolls

Scribes made pens from reeds. They wrote in black ink, using red ink to highlight parts of the text.

Carrying case for reed pens and ink

MAKING PAPER FROM PAPYRUS

1 Papyrus reeds grew all along the banks of the Nile. They were used to make sandals, ropes and boats. The Egyptians realized that they could also make a kind of paper from these reeds.

2 They cut the triangular papyrus stems into pieces about 15 centimetres long. Then they peeled off the skin and cut the pieces longways, into thin strips.

3 Next they arranged the strips in layers, first one way, then the other. They hammered the layers with a mallet, then let them dry with a weight on top.

4 The sap of the papyrus acted like a glue, binding the strips together into a sheet. After drying, any uneven parts of the surface were polished smooth with a stone. Sheets were fixed together to make scrolls. Papyrus could be cleaned and reused.

EGYPT AT WAR

Egyptian armies were formidable in battle. When Egypt was united under a strong pharaoh, its army was able to defeat almost any enemy it might meet. During the Old Kingdom, most Egyptian troops were farmers called up to fight. But during the New Kingdom, the pharaohs reorganized the Egyptian army into more efficient units. Charioteers, infantrymen and mercenaries were trained to fight together.

THE EGYPTIAN FIGHTING FORCE

The advanced skills and weapons of invading Hyksos armies during the New Kingdom forced the Egyptians to structure their armies properly. ◀ This pyramid shows how groups of soldiers were ranked and organized.

The pharaoh led important campaigns.

The general took command in the pharaoh's absence. He was often the Egyptian crown prince.

Military officers gave orders in battle.

Charioteers were often the sons of noblemen.

Their chariots were supplied by the state.

A separate division of the army organized supplies and equipment for the soldiers. Scribes kept records of the campaigns.

Footsoldiers were either professional fighters or men called up to fight during wartime. Some were mercenaries who came from abroad to fight for a living.

Some footsoldiers were bowmen; others fought with axes and daggers.

CHARIOTS INTO BATTLE

Wooden chariots were introduced into Egypt by the Hyksos between 1640 BC and 1532 BC. The chariots were fast, manoeuvrable and revolutionized Egyptian fighting. Large chariots were manned by a driver and a fighter armed with a shield and a small bow.

KEY

1 wooden chariot
2 driver
3 fighter
4 bow and arrow
5 shield
6 wrist protector

THE BATTLE PLAN

Pharaohs of the New Kingdom probably tried to fight their battles according to this plan:

1 Archers were sent forward first.

2 Light chariots would gallop up and down the enemy line attacking with arrows, in an attempt to find a weak spot.

3 Once a weak spot was found, the footsoldiers surged forward to try to force a way through the enemy line. If they failed, heavy chariots were sent in.

4 Once a gap was made, the footsoldiers and chariots would dash through to attack the enemy from the rear.

5 Light chariots would then chase away fleeing enemy troops.

WEAPONS FOR BATTLE

Bow and quiver
full of arrows with bronze tips

Bronze dagger

Short sword

Wrist cover and finger guard to protect archers from the whip of a bow

Battle axe

EGYPT'S ENEMIES

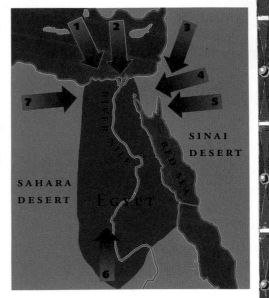

1 The Sea Peoples were made up of several tribes sweeping south from Europe and Asia during the later New Kingdom. They had powerful fleets of warships.

2 The Hittites ruled a large empire in what is now Turkey during the New Kingdom. They were the first enemy to use iron weapons, and chariots more powerful than Egyptian ones.

3 The Hyksos came from Palestine towards the end of the Middle Kingdom. In about 1650 BC they captured Lower Egypt. They were the first people to use chariots in battle.

4 The Syrians lived beyond the Sinai desert. During the New Kingdom, they were made up of several different peoples, such as the Philistines, Israelites and Amorites.

5 The Persians conquered the Egyptians in 525 BC. Their empire was one of the largest the world has ever seen, stretching from North Africa through to India.

6 The Nubians lived south of the First Cataract. They were highly skilled archers and were often hired as mercenary soldiers by the Egyptians.

7 The Libyans lived west of Egypt. They usually fought on foot and were easily defeated by Egyptian chariots.

BIGGEST BATTLES

1479 BC Battle of Megiddo
Pharaoh Tuthmosis III and 20,000 men defeat a Syrian army of 15,000 with a massive chariot charge. They capture 924 chariots, 2,238 horses and 200 suits of armour.

1288 BC Battle of Kadesh
Pharaoh Ramesses II and 5,000 men are ambushed by 3,500 Hittite chariots and 9,000 footsoldiers in Palestine. Ramesses holds off the enemy until the rest of his 20,000-strong army arrives. Details of his victory are carved onto temple walls.

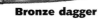

'Gold of Bravery' flies were awarded to successful battle commanders.

Egypt After the Pharaohs

After the New Kingdom Egypt entered a period of civil war and divided rule. Pharaohs and dynasties were weak and central power was lost. Egypt was attacked by the Assyrians in 671 BC and was eventually conquered by Persia. However, Egyptian culture flourished until AD c.300.

THE PERSIAN INVASION

In 525 BC the Persian Emperor Cambyses conquered Egypt. He ruthlessly ignored Egyptian traditions and gods and taxed the people heavily.

THE GREEKS

In 332 BC the Greek king Alexander the Great captured Egypt from the Persian Empire. After Alexander died, his general Ptolemy took over Egypt. Ptolemy wanted to be popular with his subjects, so he built new temples in the Egyptian style and worshipped Egyptian gods. Many cities adopted Greek styles and culture, but Ptolemy did not force the Egyptians to abandon their culture.

THE PTOLEMIES

For nearly 250 years Egypt was ruled by the descendants of the Greek general Ptolemy. The 14 pharaohs were all called Ptolemy, while most of the queens were called either Cleopatra or Arsinoe. The Ptolemies had a bloodstained history. Ptolemy IV murdered his father to gain the throne. Ptolemy VIII not only murdered his nephew, he also killed his wife! Egypt became weak as the royal family tore itself to pieces.

A coin showing Ptolemy I

ALEXANDRIA: A NEW CITY BY THE SEA

Under Ptolemy I, the new city of Alexandria on the Egyptian coast flourished. He brought many Greek scholars and artists there. A great library was built, and Alexandria became the most important centre of learning in the Ancient Greek world. Ptolemy had a large gymnasium built, which was considered the most beautiful building in the entire city. Greek games and sports such as jumping and running were introduced.

Cleopatra

The last independent pharaoh of Egypt was Queen Cleopatra VII. She took power in 44 BC by murdering her brother, Ptolemy XIV. Cleopatra was famous as a beautiful and intelligent woman. She ruled Egypt skilfully and efficiently. In 31 BC Cleopatra took the side of Mark Antony in a civil war within the Roman Empire. Mark Antony lost and Egypt became a Roman province. Cleopatra committed suicide.

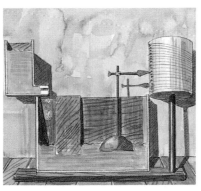

Cleopatra let poisonous snakes called asps bite her.

THE LAST YEARS OF THE PHARAOHS AT A GLANCE

671 BC Assyrians capture Memphis

660 BC Assyrians capture Thebes, Egypt becomes a province of Assyrian Empire

626 BC Egypt independent under Psammetichus I

525 BC Egypt conquered by Persian Empire

404 BC Egypt independent under Amyrtaios

343 BC Egypt conquered by Persian Empire

332 BC Persian Empire conquered by Alexander the Great

310 BC Egypt independent under Ptolemy I, general of Alexander

51 BC Cleopatra VII, last independent ruler of Egypt, comes to the throne

30 BC Cleopatra defeated by Roman Empire, Egypt becomes a province of Rome

Science and technology

During the Ptolemaic Period many Greeks came to live in Egypt. The merging of Greek thought and Egyptian skills led to a massive boom in science and technology. Ptolemy III allowed his doctor, Erasistratus, to carry out experiments on criminals who had been sentenced to death. Some of these tests were gruesome and cruel, but they added to medical knowledge.

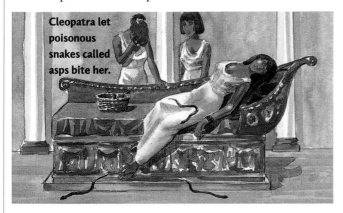

Alexandrian scholars experimented ▲ to find out whether they could power machines with water or steam. Here is a design for a water clock.

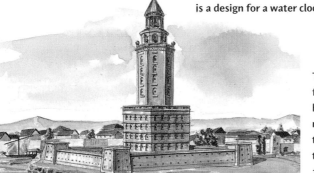

This new design for a lighthouse had bronze mirrors at the top to reflect the light. It was 120 metres tall.

THE ROMANS

Under the Roman Empire, Egypt was heavily taxed and any signs of independence were brutally crushed. The gods were still worshipped and the local people allowed to run their own lives, although Roman soldiers were stationed throughout the land. Gradually the old ways were stamped out or forgotten. By AD 350 the old Egypt had vanished.

GLOSSARY

Amulet A brooch or charm supposed to have magical powers

Canopic jars Small jars that hold the internal organs of a mummy

Cartouche An oval box in which the name of a pharaoh was written

Cataract A series of rapids and waterfalls in a river

Dynasty A family of rulers. Egyptian history is divided into thirty-one dynasties of pharaohs

Embalming Preparing a dead body with oils and spices to prevent decay

Hieratic **script** A simplified form of hieroglyphs

Hieroglyphs A form of writing using pictures to indicate words and sounds

Inundation When a river floods a large area of land

Mastaba A type of tomb with a rectangular building above ground

Mercenary A soldier who fights for another country for money

Mudbrick Bricks made by mixing mud and straw, then drying them in the sun

Mummify To preserve a dead body with chemicals and wrap it in linen bandages

Natron A natural type of salt found in the desert

Obelisk A single standing stone carved with hieroglyphs

Papyrus A reed that was used by the Ancient Egyptians to make paper

Pharaoh The king of Egypt, often thought to be a god

Pylon A tower with sloping walls erected at the entrance to temples

Sceptre A ceremonial staff used to indicate power

Scroll A long sheet of paper rolled up for easy storage

Sickle A curved knife for cutting grain

Sphinx A mythical creature with the head of a human and the body of a lion

INDEX